Goals-I

A No-Nonsense

Atul Uchil, PhD

Outskirts Press, Inc.
Denver, Colorado

Goals-Based Strategic Planning
A Non-Nonsense Practical Guide To Strategy

V2.0

Outskirts Press, Inc.
http://www.outskirtspress.com

ISBN: 978-1-4327-2330-9

Library of Congress Control Number: 2009921663

PRINTED IN THE UNITED STATES OF AMERICA

Contents

Acknowledgements

I dedicate this book to my wife **Patricia** for her unconditional support through the good and the not-so-good times and for being my inspiration, my rock.

I also have to thank Patricia for giving me my kids **Lindsey** (my daughter) and **Cory** (my son). Lindsey and Cory bring me joy and meaning and lest I forget trials and tribulations. However, they always light up my life.

My parents have been an inspiration my entire life. They are the well from which I draw my strength. They instilled in me discipline, honesty, integrity and perseverance. **Mom and Dad, I love you**.

Phil Carrai has provided me with mentorship and guidance for more than half my career. Phil stood by me as a mentor and a friend through the years. He ensured my survival in trying times by providing me with that one extra word of advice and encouragement to keep me hanging on. Phil you will always have my heartfelt gratitude and loyalty.

I thank Lieutenant Colonel Ken Beutel (US Marine Corps - Ret.) and Lieutenant Colonel Deb Beutel (US Marine Corps - Ret.) for their friendship and support over the years. They are both true patriots and both of them are recipients of the Legion of Merit medal. They are also the nicest and kindest people you will ever meet. These are people who will do anything for their friends. Patricia and I consider ourselves blessed to have you as friends. Ken & Deb, it is truly an honor to know you.

Sam Wang, a brilliant strategist and a very good friend. I thank you for your friendship and counsel. You are truly a gem among consultants and a great thought leader.

Doreen Cox, it is rare to come across an individual that possesses a strong strategic vision as well as the ability and drive to implement that vision. I thank you for your dedicated service to our great nation in defense of our nation's borders.

Major Byron Love (USAF – Ret.), your friendship and loyalty knows no bounds. You have extended your support and friendship to me; always encouraging me to go that one extra step. You are truly a man of honor.

Dennis Winkelsas, my friend and fellow member of Team Coast Guard. I thank you for lending me your grammatical skills and expertise by editing and proofreading my books for me.

Lieutenant Commander Jimmy Lewis (US Navy – Ret.), I thank you for being a good friend and a solid, down-to-earth sounding board for my ideas. I value and treasure your friendship and your counsel.

I thank Lieutenant Colonel Thomas Stuckey Jr. (US Marine Corps - Ret.) for his guidance, advice and eagle eyes. It is a distinct pleasure and honor to call you my friend.

Commander John Potts, (US Coast Guard – Ret.), I thank you for the years of guidance, advice and wisdom. All that I have achieved as a staff officer in the USCGA, I can directly or indirectly attribute to you.

Bill, Karen, Ray and Nancy Ashton, you have treated me as part of your family for the past two decades. You always accepted me for who I am through all the vicissitudes of my life. I feel proud to be associated with your family.

I cannot help but mention Kent (Big-M) Morgan, the wise old man. He is not that old but definitely wise beyond his years. His calm stoic attitude and approach has saved my bacon more than once.

No book is ever completed without the help of many people whose friendship, advice and help are critical to the completion of the project.

To all of you that I have not explicitly mentioned here, I extend my gratitude for your help and my apologies for not having your name here.

SPECIAL NOTE: I cannot thank my wife Patricia enough for putting her considerable talents as an artist and muralist at my disposal in order to conceptualize and paint the cover image for this book.

Introduction

Why am I writing a book on strategic planning?

What qualifies me as an expert on strategic planning?

I asked myself these very questions when I sat down to plan this book.

I guess I must have been satisfied with the answers because I wrote this book after all.

I know, I know. You are probably saying, "I wish this idiot will just tell me what it is and stop trying to be coy."

I bet, I may not have been one hundred percent correct, but I was pretty-darned close.

All right, I will tell you.

However, before I do, let me tell you this.

--- *I sometimes use words, language and expressions in*

my books to explain various incidents as they happened. I am not normally in the habit of using strong (foul) language. However, some incidents will loose their flavor if I try to censor them. Therefore, I apologize in advance if I offend anyone's sensibilities. That is not my intent. ---

Let us get back to the questions.

Why am I writing a book on strategic planning?

I am writing a book on strategic planning because I feel that this is an often-misunderstood field of endeavor. Strategic planning is actually very simple process and very easy to follow. I do not think there are enough books available that explain strategic planning in simple terms to the average individual. I am writing this book in the hopes of helping the readers gain an insight into the simplicity of the strategic planning process.

What qualifies me as an expert on strategic planning?

I have helped large corporations, small businesses, individuals and large Government agencies with their strategic plans. Just prior to writing his book, I helped a very large Government agency (I cannot name them here for obvious reasons) with their (2008-2013) strategic plan and their international affairs strategy.

Therefore, I feel I am qualified an expert on strategic planning.

I also need to highlight something else before you continue reading. Those of you that have read my prior books already know my writing style. I always start out by planning my book to be precisely structured treatise. I plan for well-structured chapters with surgically precise (in other words dry and drab) content.

However, after I start writing, more often than not, it seems that my passion for writing always gets the better of me. If you have read any of my prior books, you know that I only write books on topics that I am passionate about.

Very soon, I find that I have traded a lot of the planned structure for more informative real-life experiences. Many years of accumulated information, experience and knowledge, escapes the confines of my mind and drives my fingers to type words in some form of spontaneous overflow of powerful thoughts and feelings. Therefore, I end up writing an apology to the reader – post fact.

For this book, I have given up on trying to write a well-structured book. Instead, I have decided to let the flow guide me.

Several people have also told me that reading my books is akin to having a conversation with me. I guess that makes sense. Because when I am in the process of writing a book, I write as if I am having a dialog with someone sitting in front of me.

Consequently, I invite you to join me in this dialog and hope that you enjoy the conversation.

If you are looking for a well-structured book with information delivered in precise format, this may not be the best book for you. However, if you are looking for an abundance of relevant information interspersed with over almost a quarter century of real-life experiences both good and bad narrated with a lot of passion and caring, you will find this book stimulating and insightful.

I will let you be the judge!

Chapter 1
Strategic Planning

When I started writing this book on strategic planning, I realized very quickly that it would be a very short book. In fact, it turned out to be the shortest of my books to date.

The process of strategic planning is a well-defined, systematic and uncomplicated process. The difficult part is that strategic planning is extremely subjective. This leads to some very interesting people-dynamics especially during the strategic planning meetings and workshops. Not every individual reacts to large quantities of often-contradictory information, stress and or perceived frustrations in the same way.

I was moderating a strategic planning workshop for a client. Moreover, I was under the impression that all was going well. Until, one gentleman, who shall remain unnamed, (of course after this incident, I am not sure if I should still continue calling him a gentleman), stood up and informed me that he thought I was deliberately slighting him.

He then proceeded to use some choice words to describe my ancestry and what he thought I should do with myself. Yes, F-Bombs were involved.

It took an extreme amount of will power to contain myself and not to speak out what I was thinking.

I understand that this is an extreme situation. I am not implying that this will happen to you during your strategic planning process. However, I want you to be prepared for what you might potentially encounter.

No two people will have the same view on the primary elements of strategic planning (i.e. Mission, Vision, SWOT, etc.). If you are the individual moderating the strategic planning process, I recommend that you maintain a very calm and stoic attitude throughout.

It also benefits you immensely if you act purely in the role of a moderator and not as a content creator. I personally have not seen this dual-role (moderator & content creator) achieve success.

The biggest challenge in the strategic planning process is to get all the individuals to buy-in to the components of the strategic plan and to get them all on the same sheet of music.

Regarding Strategy

One of the most **common misconceptions** that I have heard repeatedly is the following: **The only way for an organization to succeed is by creating and following a strategic plan**.

Well folks, in my experience, this is not the case at all. I have seen and can recount many instances where an organization has succeeded for lengthy periods without having given any thought to strategy.

As my friend and mentor (Mr. Phil Carrai) has often said, "Even a rollercoaster will eventually arrive at its destination as long as it stays on its tracks."

I am sure there are people out there that might actually enjoy a rollercoaster ride in business. Moreover, I am not saying there is anything right or wrong with conducting your business like a rollercoaster. For who am I to judge.

Personally, if I want a rollercoaster ride, I will go to a theme park. I DO NOT want my organization to run like a rollercoaster. I prefer my business to run in a stable fashion. I seek my thrills elsewhere. That's just me!!!

PLEASE NOTE: *For the purposes of this book, I am using the word* ***'organization'*** *to define any group of people working towards a collective goal. This could refer to a team, a company, a non-profit organization, a military unit, a social club, etc.*

Managing Your Organization

There are four ways to manage an organization. Well actually, there are five! However, we will not count chaos as a means of managing so let us stick with four.

- **Managing By Crisis** – This management style is typically characterized by an unclear strategy and ineffective operations. The organization keeps careening from crisis to crisis and usually implodes in the long-term.

These organizations usually have a very high-strung and often stressful work environment. Something is always wrong and there is always a fire to put out. I personally do not like this environment. However, some individuals and groups perform exceptionally well and sometimes thrive in such environments.

- **Managing By Dreams** – A clear strategic mission and/or vision but ineffective operations typically characterize this management style. This approach usually works in the short-term. However, increasing competition makes long-term success doubtful.

  These are usually the fun organizations and tend to have very idealistic principles. Moreover, I never discount the sheer force of will of the right dreamer or group of dreamers with the right idea at the right time. I have seen some of these organizations become wildly successful far beyond anyone's expectations.

- **Managing Tactically** – This management style is typically characterized by an unclear strategy but highly effective operations. This approach usually works and can appear to be successful in the short-term and sometimes in the long-term also. However, any sudden change in the internal or external environment can make survival difficult.

If the internal and external environments remain relatively unchanged, these organizations can survive and even flourish for long periods. In addition, some types of businesses require the adoption of a tactical approach in order to achieve success.

- **Managing Strategically** – This management style is typically characterized by a clear well-defined strategy and effective operations. Almost all operational decisions support the strategic direction of the organization. The organization plans for and achieves long-term success.

  I am personally in favor of strategically managed organizations. Not that I am biased or anything, (wink! wink!), considering my core line of business. However, as a rule, these organizations generally tend to be consistent, well-organized and well-run. They seem to possess the ability to achieve consistent growth and successes.

Regarding Strategic Planning

In most organizations, the strategic planners and the senior leadership usually know much of what will go into a strategic plan even before beginning the strategic planning process. This statement applies to the operational (implementation) plans as well.

The development of a strategic plan helps to clarify the organization's plans and ensure that key leaders are all "on the same page" or "on the same sheet of music" or *<insert your favorite cliché here>*.

There are many clichés, take your pick.

Three elements are critical to strategic planning. Any strategic planning effort must at minimum address:

- The organization's interaction with its environments (internal & external)
- The allocation of resources including but not limited to capital, labor, and capacity
- The long-term issues and/or short-term issues that have long-term consequence that the organization faces

In order to accomplish the above successfully, the strategic planners and organizational leaders must have a comprehensive understanding of the internal and external entities that can influence the organization environment, and the nature of the interactions between the entities.

It also requires a comprehensive understanding of the SWOT with respect to the organization. SWOT refers to Strengths, Weaknesses, Opportunities and Threats. We will discuss SWOT in detail later in this book.

While it is important to conduct the strategic planning process using tried and true principles, it is more important that the following 'organization-specific' factors strongly influence the development of a strategic plan.

- Leadership style
- Organizational culture
- Organizational type (i.e. for-profit, non-profit, government, etc.)

- Complexity of the organization
- Size
- Target market
- Types of services provided, etc.

There are a myriad of models and approaches used in strategic planning. They include but are not limited to the following.

- Goals-based strategic planning
- Issues-based strategic planning
- Organic strategic planning
- Scenario-based strategic planning

Goals-based strategic planning focuses on the organization's mission, vision and values. This is followed by a definition of the following elements:

- Goals that support the mission and vision
- Objectives to achieve the goal
- Strategies to accomplish the objectives
- Operational plans to execute the strategies

And

- Performance measures to monitor progress

Issues-based strategic planning begins by examining the issues facing the organization, identifying strategies to address those issues, and creating action plans to implement the strategies.

Organic strategic planning begins by articulating the

organization's vision and values and creating action plans to achieve the vision while adhering to those values.

Scenario-based strategic planning begins by defining hypothetical scenarios based on perceived internal and/or external factors facing the organization and by creating action plans in response to those scenarios.

Levels of Strategic Planning

It has been a long held belief that organizations should develop multiple levels of strategic plans that support the achievement of the same basic future vision.

- Enterprise Level Strategic Plan
- Department or Division Level Strategic Plan
- Program (Project) or Initiative Level Strategic Plan

A more recent phenomenon has been to categorize the enterprise level strategic plan as the only strategic plan for the organization and the other two as operational or implementation plans. In this scenario, you have the following:

- Enterprise Level Strategic Plan
- Department or Division Level Operational (Implementation) Plan
- Program (Project) or Initiative Level Operational (Implementation) Plan

While one could make an argument to support either scenario, I personally subscribe to the latter school of thought.

However, rather than getting into a philosophical debate on semantics and trying to identify which approach is better, I am going to describe the three plans below and leave it up to the person/s creating their strategic plan to categorize them as they see fit.

We have all heard of the saying, "A rose by any other name........."

Enterprise Level Strategic plan: This is the strategic plan defined in the following chapters of this book. This is the corporate strategic plan for your organization. It should contain the organizational mission, vision, values, goals, objectives, strategies, performance measures, etc.

This plan should influence the direction of the organization, all organizational decisions and the allocation of resources and budget.

Department or Division Level Operational (Implementation) Plan: This plan details out how a specific department, division or group within the organization is going to support the Enterprise (Organizational) strategy.

This plan creates guidelines for managing a specific, area within the organization and identifies the concrete tactical steps that each area will implement in order to contribute to the organizational goals and strategies.

Program (Project) or Initiative Level Operational (Implementation) Plan: This plan details out the day-to-day activities required for carrying out the requirements of the higher level plans. These are the individual program and project plans that detail activities for that specific activity at a granular level. Programs, projects or initiatives are typically the lowest level within an organization and are directly responsible for specific operational goals.

After having said all this and most probably confused the hell out of the reader (I sincerely hope not), I think it is time for us to define what strategic planning **"is"** and equally, what strategic planning **"is not"**.

What Is Strategic Planning

Strategic planning is a very useful tool and a practical process that helps analyze the organization and its environment to strengthen the management decision-making process by providing management with the information required to recognize and address key internal and external factors that affect the business.

Whew!!! Okay, I admit, that was a mouthful. I doubt I would be able to repeat that if you asked me. So please do not try to memorize this statement.

Instead, let us examine some of the key themes that fall out of the statement above.

- It is a tool
- It is a process
- It provides information
- It helps in the decision making process

Isn't that much better and easier to remember. Let me reiterate.

Strategic planning is a tool and a process that provides information and helps in the decision making process.

Now that we have reasonably defined what strategic planning is, let is look at what it is not.

What Strategic Planning Is Not

First and foremost, strategic planning is a tool and a process. It is NOT a substitute for the exercise of judgment by organizational management (leadership).

It identifies and prioritizes the issues that may affect the organization but it does NOT tell the organizational management (leadership) what are the most important issues to address. That is left up to the judgment of the organization's senior management. Assuming that their judgment is sound, there should be no problem at all.

It identifies potential responses in the form of mitigating strategies for the issues that may face the organization but it does NOT tell the management of how they should respond to a particular issue.

REMEMBER: A chainsaw does not automatically chop down a tree. Someone skilled has to use it appropriately to accomplish that goal.

Similarly, the analysis derived from and the tools inherent to strategic planning does not make the organization perform. They support the reasoning, skills, and judgment that people bring to the organization.

Goals-Based Strategic Planning

Strategic planning anticipates the future environment but it does NOT predict future decisions. What I am trying to say here, is that just because you create a five-year plan, this does not allow you the luxury to sit around for the next four years. You must evaluate the strategic plan periodically and may have to revise it based on changes in the organization's internal or external environment.

NOTE: *Goals-based strategic planning is the most prevalent method for strategic planning. Therefore, the information in the rest of this book is discussed in reference to goals-based strategic planning.*

Hold on just a minute. What is this the title of this book? I guess the note above was unnecessary. DUH! Atul

Chapter 2

Strategic and Tactical

In order to understand strategic planning, we must first try to identify what is strategic and what is tactical. Also, notice that said:

Strategic "AND" Tactical

---NOT---

Strategic "VERSUS" tactical

Some of you are probably wondering why?

Let me tell you.

I believe that both strategic and tactical plans are equally critical to an organization's success or failure. Most successful leaders that I have met seem to have the following trait in common. They understand and utilize strategic planning to chart the course for their organization.

However, they also understand that the tactical day-to-day operations of the organization, if executed properly, make achieving the overriding strategy possible.

As far as defining "what is strategic" and "what is tactical" is concerned, the answer is very simple really.

At the most rudimentary level, **strategic** defines the **"what and why"** and **tactical** defines to the **"how."**

The strategic plan of an organization reflects the ability of its leaders to comprehend the big picture by taking into account patterns and trends, identifying ways to capitalize on potential opportunities, identifying means to mitigate anticipated issues and predicting outcomes.

Strategic issues deal with overriding mission and purpose of the organization by specifying why it exists, how it makes a difference, and where it plans to go in the future.

The tactical aspect refers to the day-to-day operations of the organization and defines how these activities ensure the achieving of strategic goals. Please see "operational plans" mentioned later in the book.

Having well defined strategic and tactical plans greatly increases the chances of success for any organization.

Chapter 3
The Strategic Planning Process

I have said before and I reiterate; the strategic planning process is more important than the final work product, usually the strategic plan document. This is because it is very important that the senior leadership team and the key staff working within an organization be on the same sheet of music with respect to the following:

- Who they are as an organization
- Where they are going

And

- How they plan to get there

Strategic planning is a means of clarifying an organization's core purpose, ensuring that its resources align to support that purpose, communicating to the organization and identifying mechanisms to monitor success in achieving that purpose.

Strategic planning should identify the following:

- Where an organization is going over the planned period (usually one to five years)
- The means by which it is going to get there
- The means of communicating the Strategic plan to the organization

And

- The mechanisms to monitor if it got there or not

Typically, the strategic planning team develops a strategic plan for the organization as a whole. Then, components of the organization develop operational plans (tactical plans) that define the activities they will perform to support the strategic plans of the organization. We shall discuss more about operational plans in a later chapter of this book. The diagram below depicts the entire strategic planning process in one snapshot.

Figure A. The Strategic Planning Process

In order to be most effective, the strategic planning process should be conducted in five stages. Each stage builds of the previous, gradually increasing the level analysis performed on the available information and the issues identified and/or analyzed in the prior stage/s.

Stage 1 – Initialization:

- Identify appropriate personnel and create the **core strategic planning team** (These individuals will work with the external consultant to accomplish all the work)
- Identify and retain an outside consultant (moderator)
- Create a work-plan that will be followed by the core team to conduct the strategic planning process
- Identify constraints to conducting the strategic planning process (if any)
- Review the existing strategic plan (if any)
- Define (or refine) the products and/or core services of the organization
- Define (or refine) the primary markets serviced by the organization
- Identify appropriate personnel and create the **extended strategic planning team** (These individuals will provide input to the strategic planning process – SWOT, etc and participate in the final strategic planning workshop)

NOTE:

1. The extended strategic planning team should include a few key individuals from all levels of the organization

2. These individuals should be known for their integrity, their ability to see the big picture, and their ability to work discretely and maintain confidentiality

- Conduct an initial meeting with senior management and the extended strategic planning team to discuss and gain concurrence on the work-plan, the strategic planning process and the expectations for the final work product

Stage 2: Analysis:

- Conduct interviews with the senior management team to identify mission, vision & values
- Consolidate the inputs received from individual senior management members to create the mission, vision and value statements for the organization
- Conduct a meeting with the entire senior management team to ensure buy-in and a common understanding of the mission, vision and values
- Distribute the mission, vision and values to the extended strategic planning team for review
- Conduct individual meetings with the members of the extended strategic planning team to gather their input on the SWOT
- Have each member identify their views on the internal strengths and weaknesses and the external opportunities and threats and facing the organization
- Identify key issues and challenges
- Validate the core products and/or services within the organization with each member of the ex-

tended strategic planning team

- Consolidate the strengths, weaknesses, opportunities and threats gleaned from the individual members of the extended strategic planning team and formulate the organizational SWOT
- Keep the SWOT realistic and focus only on the top five or ten issues identified in each area of the SWOT

Stage 3: Strategic Planning Workshop:

- Conduct the strategic planning workshop with senior management and the extended strategic planning team using the format defined below

  NOTE: The strategic planning workshop is typically a two-day process and should be facilitated by the external consultant

  Day 1

  - Review the SWOT analysis with the participants and ensure buy-in
  - Review the mission vision and value statements with the participants to ensure that they accurately reflect the intent and do not contain ambiguous words and/or statements
  - Revise the mission and vision statements if required
  - Begin the process to identify goals, objectives and strategies (you may only get through the goals on this day)

Day 2

- o Complete the identification of goals, objectives and strategies
- o Review the vision in terms of the goals and objectives to ensure that they are in alignment (revise the vision if required)
- o Create performance measures

- ♦ Once the workshop is completed, you should have all the elements required for creating your strategic plan

Stage 4: The Work Product:

- ♦ Document the strategic plan and create the final work product
- ♦ Work with designated members of senior management to create the communication plan that will be used to communicate the strategic plan both internally and externally as appropriate
- ♦ Define the format (and/or minimum requirements) for the operational plans (action plans) that will be developed by the various department heads to support the achievement of the strategic goals and objectives

Stage 5: Communication and Implementation:

- ♦ Publicize the strategic plan internally and externally in accordance with the defined communication strategy
- ♦ Work with department heads to help them document their operational plans

IMPORTANT NOTE: *The strategic plan and operational plans should be reviewed periodically and/or in the event of significant changes in the organization's internal or external environment, (i.e. changes in technology, government regulations, market place, key competitors, economy, etc.)*

Chapter 4
The Work Product

It does not take a rocket scientist to figure out that the work product resulting form the strategic planning process is an organizational strategic plan.

Some of you may probably wonder why I choose to belabor the topic by devoting an entire chapter to the work product.

I have a very good reason and here it is.

The structure of the strategic plan is just as vital as the strategic planning process. This is because the strategic plan will have a wide audience consisting of personnel from various levels within the organization and persons outside the organization. Therefore, it is important to structure that plan is such a manner that it can be distributed piecemeal. While making sure that each piece is a self-contained document that has a meaning by itself.

This can be accomplished by organizing the format of the plan in a manner that the main body of the plan can be used for general distribution within and outside the organization.

Appendices should be used for the confidential and detail-oriented information. In addition, the appendices often include information that tends to change a lot.

The structure proposed below (note the use of the word proposed) is one of the many recommended formats for a strategic plan. I personally prefer this structure.

<u>**Main Body:**</u>

- **Chapter 1 – Executive Summary:** The executive summary should be written in plain English (no technical jargon) and to a level of detail that any "outsider" should be able to read the summary and get a comprehensive understanding of the mission, vision and values of the organization
- **Chapter 2 – The Organization:** This section should briefly describe the organization as a whole. This includes its history, current state of the organization, its major products and services, major accomplishments, etc.
- **Chapter 3 – Mission, Vision and Value Statements:** This chapter details the mission, vision and value statements identified during the strategic planning process
- **Chapter 3 – Goals, Objectives and Strategies:** This chapter documents the major strategic goals and objectives and the associated strategies identified during the strategic planning process

Appendices:

- **Appendix 1 – Description of Strategic Planning Process:** This appendix documents the process used to develop the plan, the participants (i.e. the core strategic planning team, the extended strategic planning team and the senior management members who were involved in the strategic planning process), the various meetings, the format of the workshop, any major lessons learned, etc.
- **Appendix 2 – Communications Plan:** This appendix should describe the actions that will be taken to communicate the strategic plan. It should also describe the intended audiences for the plan and most importantly the content (sections) that they will be permitted to view.
- **Appendix 3 – Data used for the Strategic Planning Process:** This appendix should include information generated during the strategic planning process (i.e. SWOT analysis, competitors, technologies, marketplace, economic factors, major issues, challenges, etc.). As a result, this appendix may end up being divided into several sub-chapters.
- **Appendix 4 – Performance Management Plan:** This appendix should include the performance measures, the strategic line-of-sight, criteria for monitoring and evaluation, and frequency of monitoring the measures associated with all goals and objectives.
- **Appendix 5 – Financial and Budget Documents:** This appendix includes prior cycle's budget (with actuals), current cycle's budget, a

balance sheet or statement of financial position, etc. It should also document the resources and funding needed to obtain and the resources needed to achieve the strategic goals.

- **Appendix 6 – Operational Plans:** This appendix documents the major goals and activities to be accomplished over the next few fiscal years by the various departments in support of the strategic goals and objectives

NOTE: While the list above is certainly not exhaustive, it describes the most common elements found in strategic plans.

It is also important to understand that the strategic plan is an evolving tool and a guide to help in developing other organizational plans and in allocating resources.

The Strategic Plan should be reviewed and updated as often as necessary to stay current with changing circumstances that could potentially affect the organization's mission.

Chapter 5
Terminology

This section defines the most common terms that you will encounter during the strategic planning process.

For those of you that keep track of such things, the listing below is not in alphabetical order but rather in the order in which you are most likely to encounter them in the strategic planning process.

This is possibly the most important chapter in this book from the reader's perspective. I personally believe and tell all my clients that the strategic planning process is fairly simple and straightforward.

Understanding the terms and having a good grasp of what they represent is critical. In order to generate a good strategic plan and the associated work products, it is not sufficient to know the textbook definition of the terms. It is vital to understand the underlying purpose and intent of the work product represented by each term.

In addition, each of these terms will most likely represent a section (or appendix) in your strategic plan.

MISSION STATEMENT

The mission statement of an organization is a broad description of the nature and purpose of the business and/or the "reason for existence." It usually covers the major functions and operations of the organization and answers the following questions:

- What do we do?
- For/To whom do we do it?

And

- Why do we do it?

The mission statement should be precise and succinct. It should be an accurate representation of the organization's reason for existence. It may incorporate the target market, products/services and the geographic domain.

CAUTION: Take great care not to make your mission statement too generic or ambiguous. What may work for one organization may not necessarily be true for another.

For example:

> A mission statement that says, **"We are in the business of making money,"** is not a valid mission statement for most organizations. However, it could be the perfect mission statement for the US Mint.

Another example:

> A mission statement that says, **"We are in the Consulting Business,"** is too general. It does not define your organization specifically.
>
> The mission statement for my organization (Uchil, LLC) is – "To provide high quality specialized management and strategic consulting services to the US Federal Government and US DoD agencies."
>
> Sometimes mission statements can be very impactful one-liners'. The best example of such statement that I have found is the mission statement for WALMART. **"Saving people money so they can live better."**
>
> --- *Source http://www.walmartstores.com/7649.aspx (on December 14, 2008)*

VISION STATEMENT

A vision statement is a conceptual image of the desired future that answers the question "What do we want to be?" Vision statements should be short, memorable, idealistic, inspiring and should challenge everyone within the organization to achieve that future.

Vision statements are often confused with mission statements, but they serve complementary purposes. The most impactful vision statements typically describe outcomes that are five to ten years away.

Vision statements can be much longer than mission

statements. Their purpose is to portray an emotional message that can energize and inspire the rank-and-file of the organization.

The quality of your vision is a reflection of the quality of your organization. A powerful vision statement should stretch expectations and inspire the organization to achieve lofty goals.

I once participated in a strategic planning session led by my friend and mentor (Mr. Phil Carrai). As an ice-breaker, Phil asked us to take five minutes and think of an idea that could generate one thousand dollars ($1,000) in one month. The group came up with several ideas.

After we discussed our ideas, Phil asked us if any of those ideas could generate one million dollars ($1,000,000) over the next few years. Well, it will not come as a surprise to anyone when I say that none of the ideas presented even came close.

Phil concluded the icebreaker by saying, **"You cannot generate a million dollars by using a thousand-dollar vision."**

What an impactful statement. It is no wonder that I have such a high level of respect for Phil and the pearls of wisdom he often throws my way.

When defining your vision statement, first envision the most optimistic scenario. Then, think of something bigger and better than the most optimistic scenario that you imagined. Use this as the basis of the vision statement for your organization.

Describe your vision statement in present tense as if your organization is already there and you are merely stating how you would feel after the most optimistic scenario above is realized.

IMPORTANT NOTE: *The purpose of the vision statement is to inspire, motivate, and energize your organization.*

The vision statement for Uchil, LLC is – "We are the premier "go-to" partner for all US Federal Government Civilian and DoD agencies that facilitates their strategic planning process by providing them with the most qualified resources that embody the appropriate mix of relevant education and experience."

NOTE: The vision statement is in the present tense.

- Is Uchil, LLC there at this moment in time? --- No
  If it were, we would be revising our vision statement to reflect the next future state
- Do I believe that I will get there? --- MOST EMPHATICALLY YES

"Mission Statements" and "Vision Statements" while inherently similar and inter-dependent in nature, perform two distinctly different jobs. Therefore, your mission and vision statements have to be complimentary.

The primary difference between a mission and vision statement is that the mission statement focuses on the present state of the organization and the vision statement focuses on the future. Enough said…

VALUE STATEMENT

The value statement is one of the soft elements in the strategic planning process. It defines the values that govern the organization and the beliefs of its stakeholders.

The value statement helps define the organization's culture, priorities and the way in which it will treat its environment (including but not limited to employees, customers and society at large). Broadly defined the values are the organization's rules of professional conduct that influence both the mission and the vision of the organization.

STRATEGIC ANALYSIS

The core strategic planning team will conduct this activity during the strategic planning process. This typically includes a thorough review, of the organization's internal environment (i.e. political, social, economic and technical).

The core team will also conduct a comprehensive review of the external environment or the various driving forces in the environment, for example, competitors, changing demographics, government regulations, etc.

This information in conjunction with the SWOT should be used to revise the mission and vision. It should also be considered when developing the strategic goals and objectives.

SWOT ANALYSIS

Simply defined a SWOT analysis is an exercise that identifies the Strengths, Weaknesses, Opportunities and Threats that are currently causing or may in the near future cause an impact to your organization. SWOT is sizeable effort unto itself and is therefore addressed in a separate chapter later in this book

GOALS, OBJECTIVES AND STRATEGIES

GOALS

Goals are broad statements that define what the organization will be able to do when it achieves the desired future state.

As depicted in figure 'A' (The Strategic Planning Process), an organization's goals help bridge the gap between the current state and the future vision. Goals are qualitative statements and can be lofty ideas, using words like "robust," "adaptable," or phrases like "demonstrates industry leadership capability," etc.

A goal is the desired end-result that:

- Addresses the organization's key strategic issues
- Identifies what the organization wants to achieve
- Supports the mission and vision
- Provides a framework for creating detailed, tactical (operational) plans

And

- Is expected to remain unchanged for the for foreseeable future

OBJECTIVES

Objectives are statements of achievements that support the fulfillment of a goal.

Further defined, an objective is a specific, measurable target for accomplishing a goal that:

- Describes a specific accomplishment that meets the goal
- Focuses on expected result/s of the accomplishment
- Forms the foundation for strategies

And

- Is expected to be achieved within a pre-defined period (near term)

STRATEGIES

A strategy is a specific, high level action or approach that the organization plans to implement to achieve goals and objectives.

The Difference Between Goals and Objectives

Simply defined, the goals define where the organization wants to be and the objectives define the steps needed to get there.

- Goals are broad while objectives are narrow
- Goals maybe intangible while objectives are always tangible
- Goals could be general intentions while objectives are precise and measurable
- Goals can be lofty and abstract while objectives are concrete.

Most importantly, the objectives must be SMART. I know, you are probably wondering what I mean by 'SMART'?

SMART is an acronym, it stands for Specific, Measurable, Acceptable, Realistic and Time-bound:

<u>Specific:</u> It is difficult to know what the organization should be doing if it is asked to pursue the objective to **"increase productivity"**. It is easier to relate to this goal if it is expressed as an objective that states **"Build more computers every month".**

<u>Measurable:</u> Taking the example above one-step further, It is difficult to relate to the scope of **"Build more computers every month"**. However, it becomes a lot clearer if it is expresses as **"Increase computer production by 150 units"**.

<u>Acceptable:</u> If a division or department within the organization responsible for achieving the goal then the goal should be acceptable to that division. This can be accomplished by involving the divisional leadership in setting the goal to ensure that the division does not have any conflicting commitments.

Realistic: In addition to being specific, measurable and acceptable, it is extremely important that the goal should be realistic. For example, if the goal is to **"Increase computer production by 150 units per month"**, it is important to ensure that the division or department has the resources (i.e. staff, machinery, raw materials, etc.) required to achieve the goal.

Time-Bound: While the statement **"Increase computer production by 150 units per month"**, is specific, measurable, acceptable and realistic, it still does not address how the work is defined over the timeframe.

For example, this could mean, that the division could do nothing for the first three weeks of the month and then try to build 150 additional computers in the last week.

This goal can be better defined in terms of SMART as follows: **"Increase computer production by 3 units per day to achieve an overall increase of 150 units per month."**

While it is important to keep the SMART criteria in mind while developing the goals and objectives, it is not advisable to get too wrapped up in format at the risk of compromising the content. Content and intent is always the first priority in the strategic planning process.

Here is an example of one of the strategic goals for Uchil, LLC and the associated objectives.

Uchil, LLC Goal #2: Achieve recognition for high-quality strategic consulting services within the US Federal Government and DoD.

Uchil, LLC Objectives for Goal #2

2.1 By the end of FY2012, recruit and retain at least 10 innovative, dedicated and talented consultants, and other professionals from diverse backgrounds whose work can lead major programmatic improvement initiatives.

2.2 Support professional development in strategic and creative work.

2.3 Communicate performance expectations and accountability for job descriptions and provide uniform, constructive evaluation to one hundred percent of the staff every year.

2.4 Create, support and promote at least one Center of Excellence within each area of specialization by the end of FY-2012.

2.5 Ensure the continuous use of technology to enhance the quality of consulting services.

If you review the above carefully, you will soon realize that objectives 2.1, 2.3 and 2.4 meet the SMART criteria to a T. However, the other two do not fully meet the SMART criteria.

Does this imply that they are not valid objectives? Absolutely NOT!

Remember what I said, about trying to follow the SMART criteria but not falling hostage to the criteria. As a rule of thumb, if it makes common sense, I personally do not care if every objective meets the SMART criteria.

OPERATIONAL PLANS

These are tactical-operational plans developed by components of the organization. These plans define the specific activities that the department of division will undertake to achieve the goals defined in the strategic plan. Operational plans are defined in detail in a later chapter of this book.

PERFORMANCE MEASURES

Performance measurement is the process to track the impact of an objective, focusing on performance results (outcomes). Similar to SWOT, Performance measurement is an art and science unto itself and is addressed in a separate chapter later in this book.

Chapter 6

SWOT Analysis

As mentioned before, a SWOT analysis is an exercise that identifies the Strengths, Weaknesses, Opportunities and Threats that are currently causing or may in the near future cause an impact to your organization.

That being said, if used appropriately, the SWOT can be a powerful technique that will help your organization carve a sustainable niche in your designated market space.

Strengths and Weaknesses are factors internal to your organization while Opportunities and Threats are factors external to your organization.

Consequently, the SWOT Analysis is sometimes referred to as the Internal-External Analysis and the SWOT Matrix is sometimes called an IE Matrix Analysis Tool.

In order to carry out a SWOT Analysis, conduct one-on-

one interviews with relevant personnel across the organization. Take care to ensure that all branches, divisions and all levels of the organization are covered. Conduct these interviews in private and do not attribute the answers.

The best way to accomplish non-attribution is to have an outside consultant conduct the interviews, consolidate all the answers they received and then reveal the SWOT to the management and strategic planning team.

The use of an outside consultant in the strategic planning process serves three purposes.

1. They can act as an impartial facilitator and help achieve consensus if differing opinions or points of view should occur.
2. In the case of SWOT, knowing that the outside consultant will consolidate answers and ensure non-attribution will help people provide frank opinions that they may not otherwise disclose to persons internal to the organization.
3. Since the consultants are outsiders, they are less likely to flavor the information received with their own thoughts and/or feelings.

Coming back to the SWOT…

The designated individuals complete each section of the SWOT by answering questions as defined below. Note: these are just sample questions. They may not all be applicable to your organization. You need to develop questions that relate to your organization.

STRENGTHS

Consider these questions from an internal perspective, and from the point of view of your customers as well as your competitors. It is critical to be realistic.

For example, if all your competitors provide high quality consultants, then having high quality consultants is not necessarily a strength that is unique to your organization.

However, if all your consultants are certified in XYZ and your competitors consultants are not, then the ready availability of certified consultants is definitely an organizational strength.

The types of questions that will help identify strengths are:

- What do you do better, cheaper, faster than anyone else does?
- What advantages does your organization possess?
- What resources are unique do your organization possess?
- What factors differentiate your organization from others?

Some examples of Strengths are:

- Your Organization's specialization or expertise
- Any new, innovative products, services or techniques that your organization possesses
- Favorable geographic location

- The quality of the work product that your organization delivers
- Other aspects of your organization that add value to your products or services

WEAKNESSES

Similar to Strengths, consider these questions from an internal perspective, and from the point of view of your customers as well as your competitors.

It is vital to be realistic in the assessments of your weaknesses during the strategic planning phase and face any unpleasant truths as soon as possible. This will give you the opportunity to develop a strategic plan that could address and mitigate these weaknesses.

The types of questions that will help identify weaknesses are:

- What products, services, and processes of your organization would you improve if you had full autonomy?
- What would your clients most likely describe as weaknesses within your organization?
- What internal factors contribute to lost sales opportunities in competitive situations?

Some examples of Weaknesses are:

- Lack of expertise that your competitors possess
- Undifferentiated products or services (i.e. you are no different from your competitors)
- Unfavorable geographic location

- The lack of quality in the work product that your organization delivers (whether factual or perceived – sometimes the perception lack of quality is more damaging)
- Unfavorable reputation with your former clients

OPPORTUNITIES

Consider opportunities from an external perspective, and from the point of view of your customers as well as your competitors.

Having identified the strengths and weaknesses, look at them and think of ways to create opportunities by:

- Eliminating weaknesses within your organization and/or
- Capitalizing on the strengths that your organization possess

The types of questions that will help identify opportunities are:

- Where opportunities are available to your organization today?
- Are there any trends or other changes that might present future opportunities?

  These trends may include but are not limited to the following:

  1. Changes in technology
  2. Changes in government policy related to your field

3. Changes in the economy (both global and local as applicable)
4. Other Local events

Some examples of Opportunities are:

- A developing technology
- A developing market (both local and global)
- Mergers, joint ventures or strategic alliances
- Changes in tax regulations
- Changes in import/export regulations
- A market left vacant by a competing organization

THREATS

Similar to opportunities, consider threats from an external perspective, and from the point of view of your customers as well as your competitors.

The types of questions that will help identify threats are:

- What are your competitors doing that might give them an advantage in the market place?
- What obstacles do you organization face?
- Are the required technologies for your products or services changing?
- Is changing technology threatening your position?
- Are any proposed changes in Government regulations inhibitors to your organizations ability to flourish?
- Does your organization have excessive debt or cash-flow problems?

- Could any of your weaknesses (in the weakness section above) seriously threaten your business?

Some examples of Threats are:

- A new competitor enters the market place
- Competitors are able to provide similar products and/or services at lower rates
- A competitor has developed a new, innovative product or service
- One or more competitors have merged or formed a strategic alliance
- Changes in tax regulations
- Changes in import/export regulations

SWOT Do's and Don'ts

The SWOT analysis can be very subjective. Therefore, it is essential that you are comprehensive and consistent in the way you apply it. Two people will very rarely come-up with the same responses to the SWOT questions.

If you are the person responsible for consolidating the SWOT, you might find the following guidelines useful.

- Only accept well-defined and verifiable statements. (For example – Our rates are too high vs. We charge $150 per our and our closest competitors charge $135 per hour).
- Prioritize the various statements in each area so that only the most significant factors become factors for consideration as you progress in the strategic planning process.
- Make sure that all factors that make the final

SWOT are considered during later stages of the strategic planning process.

- Apply the SWOT at the appropriate level. (For example, if your organization has two distinct lines of business, apply the SWOT to each line of business, rather than for the organization as a whole. The latter will lead to a vague SWOT and not be very useful during the later stages of the strategic planning process.)
- Supplement it with other tools – if applicable. TOWS analysis is extremely similar. It simply looks at the negative factors first in order to turn them into positive factors.

You can also apply the SWOT analysis to your competitors. This can provide you with invaluable insight on how and where you should compete.

Last but not the least - Do not get hung up on the SWOT too much. It is just another step in the overall strategic planning process.

The SWOT Matrix:

Some purists believe that the SWOT should be depicted in the form of a matrix as shown below. I personally believe that the information is more important than how it is depicted and I do not care if it is written as paragraphs, bullet points, matrix, or on the back of a cocktail napkin.

Just as long as the information is captured accurately and is used throughout the strategic planning process.

Strengths	Weaknesses
Opportunities	**Threats**

Chapter 7
Performance Measurement

Performance Measurement is vital to the success of organizations. Without accurate performance measurement, an organization cannot judge where it was, where it is, and most importantly, where it is going.

Therefore, performance measurement is a fundamental requirement and an integral part of strategic planning and strategic management.

The performance measurement methodology defined below is a means for providing common measurement criteria throughout the organization. If used appropriately, it provides corporate management with tools and information that will help them manage the organization at a strategic level.

It also provides a means to measure the success of strategic initiatives and their impact in terms of achieving organizational goals and objectives. The performance measurement methodology accomplishes this by identifying the input, output and outcome measures relevant to achieving the strategic goals and objectives that are defined in the organization's strategic plan.

The performance measurement methodology further helps management articulate the cause-effect relationship between inputs, outputs and outcomes. This linkage from inputs to outputs to outcomes is called a strategic line-of-sight.

The performance measurement framework can assist management in the following ways:

- It creates a clear strategic line-of-sight that links performance measures to strategic goal and objectives.
- It helps generate relevant measurements that improve organizations strategic decision making

Performance measurement is the use of statistical evidence to measure progress toward SMART organizational goals and objectives. When you get to this step in the strategic planning process, you will develop performance measures for each of the strategic objectives.

Input, Output and Outcome measures should be identified along with current baselines and expected targets. The focus on strategic objectives and the establishment of a line-of-sight is the key to identifying truly strategic measurements.

Therefore, for each measure you need establish the following:

- Type of measure (whether it is an input, output or outcome)
- The tie in to the strategic plan (i.e. what strategic objective and corresponding goal that the measure supports)
- The baseline (current state)
- The target (planned improvement to the baseline by fiscal year)
- The strategic line-of-sight

There are many techniques for defining and establishing the strategic line-of-sight. I personally prefer a technique called the "So What" Analysis Technique

The "So What" Analysis Technique:

This is essentially a bottom up approach. When you are following this process, you lead your team through an analysis and decomposition of the problem starting with the possible solution/s and working out the impacts that they will have towards achieving the stated goal.

The reason this technique is known as the "So What" technique is that you literally ask the question "so what?" at each stage until you arrive at the final outcome.

The structure of this exercise should be as follows:

Statement of Goal/s: The first step is to work with the workshop participants (extended strategic planning team and the senior management team) to describe (*in simple language*) the results that they hope to achieve in support of this goal. This is the goal and objective for which you are developing the performance measures.

Inputs: The second step is to work with the workshop participants to identify the potential solutions that they feel will help them achieve the desired goal.

Outputs: The third step is to work with the workshop participants to identify potential process impacts that each solution will produce.

Outcomes: The final step is to identify the outcome/s that will result from the proposed inputs and their resulting outputs.

Example:

Statement of Goals: The border is not adequately protected. I have been tasked with safeguarding the border against terrorism

Potential Objectives:
I could do so by erecting fences (Objective 1) or by increasing the number of guards (Objective 2)

Objective 1

I put up miles of fences. - **(Input)**

[So what?]

This will make it harder for individuals that are trying to get across the border illegally. - **(Output)**

[So what?]

They will either try to get in legally or try to get in at another spot. - **(Output)**

[So what?]

If I put up enough fences, I will be able to protect the border and reduce illegal immigration. - **(Outcome)**

Objective 2

I station guards at regular intervals. - **(Input)**

[So what?]

The guards will identify individuals trying to enter the border illegally and stop them. - **(Output)**

[So what?]

They will either try to get in legally or try to get in at another spot. - **(Output)**

[So what?]

If I station enough guards, I will be able to protect the border and make it difficult for terrorists to cross the border illegally. - **(Outcome)**

NOTE:

1. Each input could lead to one of more outputs and each output could lead to one or more outcomes.

2. Each statement above should be converted to a measure. For example, I station guards at regular intervals is great for the exercise. However, the performance measure could be, **"The number of guards stationed per mile of border in XYZ region."** Similarly, the outcome measure in the exercise could be, **"The overall percentage of border that has adequate guards stationed at regular intervals."**

I personally believe that it is better to have fewer targeted and meaningful measures rather than a large number of measures that do not necessarily measure the right things.

I am reminded of a story here. I often use this while conducting performance management workshops to emphasize the importance of adopting meaningful measures.

Here it is:

> A priest and a New York cab driver end up at the pearly gates at the same time. St. Peter greets them and informs them that they will each get a dwelling in which they will spend eternity.
>
> The catch is that the size of this dwelling will be proportional to the extent to which each of them caused people to remember God when they were on earth.
>
> St. Peter shows the priest to a modest home. At this time, the priest says, "St. Peter, if I get such a modest home after preaching the word of God for the past 40

years, I wonder what kind of shack the cabbie will get."

St. Peter says, "You are wrong priest." "The cabbie actually receives a large palatial mansion."

The priest is thoroughly perplexed. He asks St. Peter to explain the discrepancy.

St. Peter says, "There is no discrepancy priest."

"When you preached to your congregation, at least 25% of the congregation fell asleep, another 25% zoned out, 50% of them prayed to God with you."

"On the other hand, every single person (i.e. 100% of the people) that ever got in this cabbie's cab prayed to God very sincerely."

Quality Performance Measures:

How do you recognize good performance measures? Some of the criteria that are common to meaningful performance measures are listed below.

- They are explicitly defined in terms of the unit of measure, frequency of measurement and expected results (targets)
- They promote the measurement of accomplishments rather than the measurement of the quantity of work performed
- They provide a mechanism for management to monitor if the strategy is working
- They ensure measurement of the right things

- They focus the organization's attention on the factors that impact success

The final word on performance measures is that less is definitely more. Make certain that your measures are meaning full and accurately reflect the strategic line-of-sight.

Chapter 8
Operational Plans

An operational plan is derived from the strategic plan, and is a detailed action plan to accomplish the goals and the objectives defined in the strategic plan.

The operations plan should, at minimum, describe:

- Short-term business tactics that will be adopted by the specific department or division in support of the strategic plan
- How a strategic plan will be put into operation within that department or division
- The basis and justification for the annual operating budget of the department or division

The operational plan should be in the form of an annual plan that is revised every year depending on the budget cycle and fiscal year followed by the organization.

It is important to note that the operational plan should be specific to your department of division. Not all departments require the same level of complexity when it comes to the operational plan.

Your operational plan should communicate the following in a comprehensive manner:

- How you are going to deliver the product or service that is the responsibility of your department
- What are you and/or your staff is going to be doing on a daily basis to achieve the performance targets

Some of the sections (chapters) that are most common to the operational plan are defined below:

Major Goal – This is a specific goal/s from the strategic plan that pertains to your department or division

Objective – These are objectives from the strategic plan that are associated with the goal and that pertain to your department or division

NOTE: Just because a goal applies to your division, this does not mean that all its associated objectives also apply.

Strategy – These are strategies from the strategic plan that pertain to the objectives relevant to your department of division

Actions – These detail the specific day-to-day actions that your department will undertake to accomplish the strategy

Responsibility – This defines who in your department is going to perform these actions and who is going to manage the performance of these actions

Timeline – This is the timeline by which the actions will be completed to produce desired results

Resources – This section details what resources (people, space, materials, supplies, etc.) you need to achieve the task

Budget – This is the anticipated annual cost of the resources identified above

Outcome – This defines the result that you hope to achieve as a result the completion of the actions defined above

Performance Measures – Each objective will have one or more performance measures that provide a clear and unambiguous measure of performance. The measures will provide both measurement and accountability to the activities that result from the plan.

Monitoring The Operational Plan

- It is important to evaluate the entire operational plan at regular intervals throughout the year.
- Performance targets should be monitored monthly or quarterly (depending on the nature of your business). This will help you identify if the action plans that have been set are on track to achieving targets. If targets were not achieved, it

is necessary to analyze the 'Whys' and 'Why Not's" in order to develop a new plan of action or alter the existing one.

- Update and evaluate your budget monthly by comparing planned against actual. If your actual defers from your planned, it is necessary to analyze the 'Whys' and 'Why Not's" in order to develop a revised budget.
- Remember that you will create a new operational plan every year.

Chapter 9

Do's, Do Not's and Lessons Learned

Honestly folks! I could not think of a good name for a chapter that would capture the lessons I have learned through countless strategic planning sessions. I also could not think a way to organize the information. Therefore, I just decided to capture it in a disjointed fashion in this chapter.

I recommend to the reader that they not discount this chapter. The information herein will tie most of the other chapters together and help you gain a better understanding of the strategic planning process.

You may also have some "AH HA" moments if you have already conducted and/ or participated in a strategic planning session. If you have not, you are most likely to have the "AH HA" moment when you participate in a strategic planning session.

DO'S

- DO commit to the strategic process completely.

Once you decide that your organization needs to develop a strategic plan, make a total commitment to the planning process. Be prepared to provide the Core Team with time, resources and access to information and personnel as appropriate.

- DO be selective especially when completing the SWOT and identifying the most important strategic factors. Make certain that they are tailored toward your particular specific needs, culture, environment and the nature of your business.
- DO remember that your strategic plan is both an internal and external document. Make certain that you create the document with appendices so that it can be distributed in pieces (see the chapter on work product). Otherwise, you may inadvertently end up giving away competitive or confidential information outside your organization.
- DO monitor the performance measures at regular pre-planned intervals to ensure that the strategic goals and objectives are being met.
- DO collect regular feedback from participants too ensure that they understand and agree with the planning process. If not, find out what they do not like and how it could be done better.

DO NOT'S

- Even though strategic planning is a disciplined process, DO NOT expect it to flow smoothly from one step to the next. It is a creative process, and you will often find new analysis and information uncovered in the current week of planning may override decisions that we made in the prior week.

- DO NOT assume that the strategic planning process is a one-size fits all methodology. You should adapt and personalize the planning process to suit the specific needs of your organization.
- DO NOT try to create one plan that covers the strategic and tactical elements for the entire organization. It is better to have an overarching strategic plan and several operational plans that may or may not be appendices to the strategic plan.
- If any individual or individuals do not buy-in to a certain aspect of the plan, DO NOT proceed from that step until consensus has been achieved. Remember, at the end of the process, all the planners need to be on the same sheet of music.

LESSONS LEARNED AND MISCELLANEOUS STUFF

1. When should an organization conduct strategic planning?

There is no simple answer to this question. The timeframe for performing the strategic planning process depends on the nature and needs of the specific organization and its immediate external environment.

Here are some scenarios that definitely necessitate strategic planning.

- The organization should undertake strategic planning at its inception. In this case, the strategic plan should be an integral part the overall business plan.
- The organization should undertake strategic planning in preparation for a new major venture. For example, when developing a new product line, planning a new acquisition, creating a new division, expanding into a new market, etc.
- The organization should undertake strategic planning whenever a major internal or external change occurs. For example, change in finances, change in marketplace, change in regulations, change in key personnel, etc.
- Last but not the least; the organization should undertake strategic planning whenever a major change in strategic direction is envisioned. You are probably saying DUH! Atul! That is self-evident. You will be surprised at how often clients have asked me if they could use their old strategic plan to fit their new circumstances.

It is advisable to perform **periodic updates to the strategic plan**. Once again, the frequency of this activity depends on the exact nature of your business.

- Planning should be carried out frequently in organizations that are in a rapidly changing operating environment. In this situation, comprehensive planning should be performed once a year. By comprehensive, I mean planning that defines and/or revises mission, vision, values, SWOT, goals, strategies, objectives, etc).

- If the organization is in a reasonably stable operating environment, comprehensive planning should be performed once every three to five years. However, these organizations should still perform a mini planning session every year to review and revise the current plan. It is particularly important to review the performance measures and revise or update targets. Depending on the performance measures, it may become necessary to change some objectives also.
- Operational plans on the other hand should be updated every year. It is recommended that the progress of the operational plan be reviewed at least once a quarter. Again, the frequency of review depends on the extent of the rate of change within the operating environment.

2. Should you use an outside consultant?

The short answer to this question is yes. Don't, get me wrong; I am not trying to drum up business here (unless, of course, you are a large federal agency).

I strongly recommend using an outside consultant as an impartial facilitator and moderator. As discussed on in prior chapters of this book, strategic planning is a very subjective process and can be easily derailed.

An impartial facilitator that can act as a moderator

and not a content generator will enable you to keep on track.

Your outside consultant is someone who is not likely to have strong predispositions about the organization's strategic issues and ideas.

Here are some other scenarios that might necessitate you to consider using an outside consultant

- There appears to be large gap between the management and the staff about and current organizational issues or between various divisions and departments within the organization.
- Your organization has never been through a strategic planning exercise.
- You have been through strategic planning previously bit it was not successful.
- There is no one in the organization who can be a strong impartial facilitator and moderator. NOTE: If you have such an individual within your organization, you will find that they are almost always also viewed as contributors to the strategic plan. Remember what I said about the pitfalls of a dual-role (contributor & facilitator).
- Senior management believes that an inside facilitator will either inhibit participation from others. Remember what we discussed about non-attribution of the SWOT statements.

3. **Why is the planning process equal to or more important than the work product?**

   Since most of us are action oriented, a very common mistake in the strategic planning process if to place primary emphasis strategic plan work product.

   Remember folks, this is just a document. The real benefit of strategic planning is the planning process itself.

   During the strategic planning process, many participants learn a great deal from ongoing analysis, reflection, discussion, debates and dialogue.

   Assuming that your participants are, people who will eventually be responsible for implementing some or all aspects of the strategic plan, you gain their invaluable buy-in to the organization's mission and vision.

4. **What is the typical schedule for strategic planning?**

   In the most likely scenario, it should take roughly two months from the time the Core Strategic Planning and the Extended Strategic Planning teams are formed before you have the work product.

   Various factors will influence this timeline. These include but are not limited to the following:

   - This is the first strategic planning for your organization

- The process does not have management buy-in and support
- The size of your organization
- The time that the Core Team is devoted to the strategic planning project

5. What is the perfect process for strategic planning?

I have a short answer but most of you are not going to like it. There is no perfect way to conduct a strategic planning process.

I recommend that you not be concerned about finding the "perfect way" to conduct the strategic planning exercise. When you start the process, you will soon realize that every individual has his or her own interpretation of the mission, vision, SWOT, etc.

Moreover, If you try to read books on strategic planning, you will realize that every expert (or author) has their own particularly interpretation of the activities in strategic planning. I have defined several major activities and steps in the strategic planning process based on my experiences and expertise.

Other authors may have different names for these major activities. They might even recommend conducting them in a different order.

Does this make anyone right or wrong? I do not think so. As mentioned earlier, Strategic planning is a very subjective exercise. One of the major goals of the process should be to get all your leaders and impact players on the same sheet of music and secure their buy-in. The document itself will then become secondary.

6. **What are the benefits of strategic planning?**

Here is another answer that you will not like. I think that there are no real benefits to strategic planning. Now, before you start planning my lynching party, let me explain.

I have heard others say some or all of the following:

- Strategic planning will help you to build a vision for the future of your organization
- Strategic planning will allow you to recognize opportunities emerging from today's business environment and prepare you to take advantage of them.
- Etc., etc., etc.

Do you want to hear what I say to all these statements?

I say "Bullllllllshit!"

Strategic planning in itself is nothing. Yes, you may generate a great plan with a great mission, vision, values. You may even identify all possible strengths and opportunities. You may go a step further and plan for mitigating all weaknesses and threats. SO WHAT!!!

If you do not implement your strategic plan, it is just some wasted sheets of paper that will sit on a shelf somewhere gathering dust.

One of the most frequent complaints that I hear about the strategic plan is that it ends up collecting dust on a shelf and that the organization ignores the invaluable information captured in the strategic plan.

Therefore, the better questions to ask here are:

- How should I communicate and implement my strategic plan?

And

- What are the benefits of properly implementing the strategic plan?

Let me tell you.

7. How should I communicate and implement my strategic plan?

Here are some guidelines that will help you communicate and implement your strategic plan.

- Document and distribute the plan to the entire organization and consider inviting review input from all. NOTE: Make certain that appropriate levels within the organization receive the appropriate copy of the plan. Remember the appendices discussed in the "Work Product" chapter of this book. You do not want your balance sheet or budget to end up in the wrong hands.

- Management support of the plan is a major driver to the plan's implementation. Make certain that all senior leaders mention and discuss the plan at every opportunity (both formally and informally) with the staff.
- When conducting the planning process, involve the people who will be responsible for implementing the plan. They can be part of the Core Strategic Planning Team or the Extended Strategic Planning team. It does not matter. They will embrace the plan as long as they feel they have contributed to it in some meaningful way.
- Use a cross-functional team. Make sure that all levels of the organization are represented. This will not only ensure that the plan is realistic and collaborative, it will also greatly reduce if not totally eliminate the "It was created by management and I have to follow it syndrome."
- Ensure the goals and objectives are SMART (Specific, Measurable, Acceptable, Realistic and Time-bound).
- Portray performance measures as "carrots" rather than as "sticks."
- Decompose the overall strategic plan into smaller operational plans at the Department level and at the more granular program/project level. This will make the strategic plan more realistic and an integral part of the staff's day-to-day activities.

- Specify and communicate the implementation roles and responsibilities. Make sure everyone understands the fundamental question. "Who does what and why?"

Now to answer the second question.

8. What are the benefits of properly implementing the strategic plan?

The key to success is in the effective implementation of the plan. Organizations that do a good job of developing and implementing their strategies can create a competitive edge.

While there are many very real ancillary benefits of properly implementing the strategic plan, they all fall under the umbrella of the primary benefit that is to optimize the organization's potential through the formulation and realization of an appropriate future vision.

Some of the most common ancillary benefits are listed below.

- Provides a road map to show where the company is going and how to get there
- Develops a sense of security among employees that comes from better understanding of the changing environment and the company's ability to adapt
- Helps clearly define the purpose of the organization and establishes realistic goals

and objectives consistent with that mission and vision in a defined timeframe

- Focuses organizational attention on the important things by properly allocating resources to those activities that provide the most benefit
- Helps identify the impact that the changing operating environment is having on the organization and defines the needed changes in direction
- Fosters better communications with personnel both inside and outside the organization
- Promotes better internal coordination of activities
- Develops a frame of reference for budgets and short-range operating plans
- Provides an awareness of the changing environment as a foundation for needed change
- Highlights awareness of the organization's potential in light of its strengths and weaknesses
- Provides means to ensure the most effective use of the organization's resources by focusing the resources on the strategic goals and objectives
- Provide a base from which progress can be measured and establish a mechanism for informed change when needed
- Provides clear focus of organization resulting in increased productivity from increased efficiency and effectiveness
- Bridges the gap between staff and management (leadership)

About the Author

Dr. Atul Uchil is an entrepreneur, consultant and author embodying over twenty-three years of management experience.

Dr. Uchil is an accomplished, results-driven executive with a proven track record of building and growing professional service organizations and demonstrated career success directing complex, multi-million dollar consulting engagements for government and commercial clients. As an imaginative, disciplined, results-oriented leader, he effectively creates teams and processes to reduce costs and drive profitability.

Dr. Uchil has extensive DoD, Civilian-Federal, Commercial, and International experience. Prior to founding Uchil, LLC, Dr. Uchil spent over eighteen years in a variety of senior management roles at several large consulting organizations including Accenture and MCC.

Uchil, LLC offers customized motivational training seminars tailored to the specific needs of the organization and various levels of management (Jr., Mid., Sr., and Exec.) These seminars usually focus on one or more of the following subjects: Management, Leadership, Relationship Selling, Processes and Methodology.

Uchil, LLC also offers business coaching and advice for entrepreneurs and startups. This includes but is not limited to, advice and coaching on management strategy, marketing, sales, financial planning, structuring for profitability, core competency identification and development and plans for growth.

In addition to his PhD in Business Administration, Dr. Uchil also holds an MBA in Consulting Operations Management, a BSEE in Electrical Engineering and a Diploma in Electronics and Telecommunications Engineering. Dr. Uchil's doctoral degree is apostilled by US Secretary of State, General (Ret.) Colin L. Powell and bears his signature and seal.

Dr. Uchil's Certifications and affiliations include but are not limited to the following:

- Lifetime member of the Chartered Institute of Professional Management (CIPM)
- Lifetime member of Armed Forces Communications and Electronics Association (AFCEA)
- Lifetime member of the National Defense Industrial Association (NDIA)
- Member of the Institute of Electrical and Electronics Engineers (IEEE)
- Dr. Uchil serves on the Board of Advisors/Directors for several small/emerging businesses and not-for-profit organizations

Dr. Uchil also serves in the United States Coast Guard Auxiliary as a Senior Staff Officer and is a USCG certified instructor for Public Education and Boating Safety

In addition to many research papers and articles, Dr. Uchil has published several books that are available at Amazon.com, Barnes & Noble, Ingram, Baker & Taylor, Borders, BooksAMillion, Bertram Books UK, Gardners UK, Alibris and many other respected and recognized national and international book retailers.

Dr. Uchil resides in Virginia Beach, VA with his wife Patricia, a talented artist and muralist. They have two grown children a daughter (Lindsey) and a son (Cory).

You can find more information about Uchil, LLC at http://www.uchil-llc.com.

Other Books

By the Author

- **Uchil, A**. "Relationship Selling: The Fine Art OF Consultative Sales" (2007) Outskirts Press, Inc. **ISBN:** 9781432715007

  Everyone has heard the following: People like to buy - People hate being sold or being forced to buy - People buy from people that they like and trust.

  Therefore, it stands to reason that if you are the person your clients trust they will buy from you without you having to sell them anything. How then do you become the trusted advisor to your clients? How do you establish and maintain long-term relationships? This book reveals the best kept secrets of successful relationship selling and is a must-read for every consultant and sales professional.

- **Uchil, A**. "The Corporate America Survival Handbook: A Cornucopia of Essential Information" (2005) Outskirts Press, Inc. **ISBN:** 9781598000942

THE CORPORATE AMERICA SURVIVAL HANDBOOK is deliberately narrated in a format that lets the readers go to whatever section they need and read it independently of other sections.

This book is a powerful tool, providing information on a wide variety of topics including, security clearances, the job market, resume writing, patents, trademarks and much more.

This book does not contain any magical formula for success - it is mostly common sense. However, this book gives the reader many invaluable insights into Corporate America that most people do not know.

As the saying goes, "Common sense in an uncommon degree is what the world calls wisdom."

- **Uchil, A**. "Consulting: A Job Or A Lifestyle." (2005) Outskirts Press, Inc. **ISBN:** 9781598000640

  CONSULTING: A JOB OR A LIFESTYLE is comprehensive research into the life of persons that choose consulting as a career. It details the pros and cons including the lifestyle sacrifices that are an integral part of consulting.

- **Uchil, A**. "I Opted Out: The Chronicles Of A Rat Race Junkie." (2005) Outskirts Press, Inc. **ISBN:** 9781598000713

  I OPTED OUT; narrated in the form of a pseudo-autobiography, takes a poignant and satirical look at the impact of the corporate rat race on the personal life of an individual that is addicted to his work.

Today's society often parades the term 'workaholic' as a catch phrase or a badge of honor. Few recognize that addiction to work can be as dangerous as addiction to drugs or alcohol. The author presents this material in a humorous manner where possible to lighten the burden of reading, while taking care not to let humor dilute the gravity of the message.

CPSIA information can be obtained
at www.ICGtesting.com
Printed in the USA
LVOW12s2328160717
541594LV00001B/15/P